MAGNA FAMILY
LIBRARY

CARD
AND
CONJURING
TRICKS

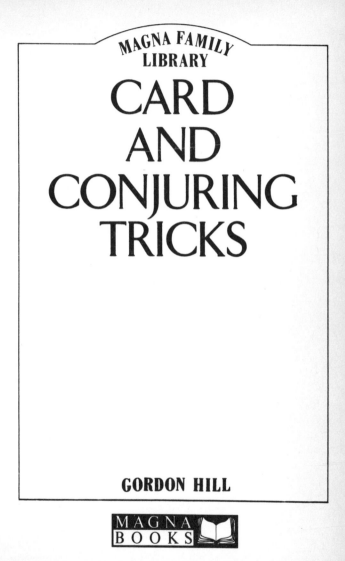

MAGNA FAMILY
LIBRARY

CARD
AND
CONJURING
TRICKS

GORDON HILL

MAGNA
BOOKS

First published in the UK
1989 by Ward Lock
a Cassell Imprint
Villiers House, 41/47 Strand, London, WC2N 5JE

This edition has been produced in 1995 for Magna Books,
Magna Road, Wigston, Leicester, LE18 4ZH, UK

For further information about Magna Books please contact:
Magna Books,
Magna Road, Wigston
Leicester LE18 4ZH, UK

ISBN 1-85422-857-9

Typeset by Columns of Reading Ltd

Printed and bound in Finland

CONTENTS

INTRODUCTION

None of the tricks in this book is difficult to do (although some may need a bit more practice than others). Unfortunately it is sometimes hard to understand a trick from written instructions since the magician is often doing one thing while pretending to do another. The best way to understand the tricks in this book is to get the various items required and then to go through the movements as you read the instructions.

Red, White and Blue on page 72 is a good example of this. On paper it looks rather complicated but it is really easy to do.

You will, from time to time, come across the words 'You are now ready to perform' after the secret of the trick has been explained. Do not take this too literally. You are not ready to perform at this stage. You are ready to practise the trick and that is all. This holds true for every trick. You must be able to do the trick properly before you show it to anyone. If you do not practise in private and keep practising until you can do the trick perfectly, you will have wasted your time in reading this book.

There is a lot more to any trick than the mere mechanics. The real secret of a successful performance lies in not how it is done but how the magician presents it. Entertainment value is much more important than the secret.

The tricks in this book range from simple to slightly advanced. Those which are easiest to do will be found in the first section. But just because they are easy, do not dismiss them. As said before, it is not the secret but the way you do the trick that is most important. Even simple tricks can be made to look good if you spend time perfecting your performance.

If you have had no previous experience of conjuring, you might think that some of the tricks are so simple they would not possibly fool anyone. Try them and you will see for yourself how easy it is to fool people with even the most elementary of tricks.

The important thing is to have self-confidence. This comes from practice, and from experience. Certainly, you will sometimes have tricks go wrong – that happens to every magician. But please do not let that deter you. Keep practising the routines, keep on performing and you will gradually get better and better, until one day you will become an expert magician.

TRICKS TO
GET YOU STARTED

POSTCARD PUZZLER

Tell your audience that you are going to walk through a postcard.

They will not believe you – until you go ahead and do it!

Fold the postcard in half lengthwise. Cut slits from the fold up towards the top edges, stopping just short of the edge, as shown.

Now make cuts downwards between the first cuts, as shown.

In actual practice, you should make more cuts than are shown in the illustrations. The more cuts you make the easier the trick becomes.

Open out the card and cut along the central crease from the last to the first cut, as indicated by the dotted line.

Carefully open out the card and you will find that it is now large enough to go over your body.

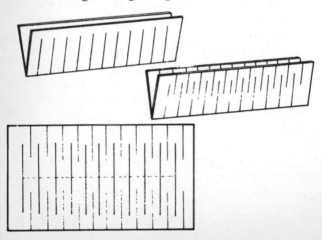

THE ANSWER IS ...

Ask someone to think of a number. This number has then to be multiplied by two. Twelve is added to the answer, which is then divided by four. Any remainder should be ignored.

The spectator is next asked to subtract half of his original number from the result he has obtained. If the original number was odd, any remainder is ignored.

Now tell him that the number he has arrived at is three.

You know the result in advance because the answer is always three!

Here is an example:

Think of a number	15
15 multipled by 2	30
30 plus 12	42
42 divided by 4	10
10 less half of 15 (7)	3

If you want to vary the result for a repeat showing, change the number to be added. This, divided by four, will provide the answer to subsequent calculations.

RUBBER PENCIL

This trick is not much more than an optical illusion. To the audience it appears that the pencil is made of rubber, whereas it is, of course, wooden and perfectly solid.

Hold the pencil near one end between the thumb and forefinger of the right hand. About an inch of the pencil should extend to the right of the hand, and the rest of the length towards the left.

Hold the pencil loosely and then move your hand up and down so the pencil rocks between your fingers.

BAFFLING BOOMERANGS

For this trick you will need two curved pieces of wood or card. Both shapes should be exactly the same size.

It is a good idea to paint each of them a different colour. We will assume that one is red and the other white.

Hold the red one above the white one. It appears that the white is the longer of the two.

Now hold the white above the red. It now looks as if the red is the longer.

Put the red boomerang back on top and the white becomes the longer again.

To make both boomerangs look the same size put them together side by side.

The trick is really a simple optical illusion so it is a good idea to pretend to stretch each of the boomerangs in turn to bring about the apparent changes. This makes the performance appear more magical.

IT'S A SNIP

Although not quite magic in the accepted sense, this little stunt appears quite amazing.

You drop a strip of paper from your left hand. As it flutters to the ground you lunge at it with a pair of scissors. You are so skilful that you manage to cut a neat piece from one end of the paper.

Your audience will believe you have spent many long hours practising this astonishing stunt, but it is accomplished by trickery.

Before your performance, you secretly place a small piece of paper between the scissor blades – and that is all there is to it!

Hold the scissors in your right hand and the strip of paper in your left.

Drop the strip of paper and lunge forward with

the scissors. Snip the scissors open and shut as you do so. This releases the small piece of paper, and it looks as though you have cut it from the long strip.

EXPANDING HOLE

Fold a sheet of paper. In the centre of the fold, cut a hole about the size of a 5p coin.

Show the unfolded paper and a 10p coin to your spectators and point out that the coin is much larger than the hole. Now state that you will pass the coin through the hole without tearing the paper.

It sounds impossible but this is how you do it:

Fold the paper in half; then place the coin inside the fold. Hold the paper by the corners and lift them upwards and towards each other.

To everyone's surprise the coin will appear in the hole and will eventually drop through it!

RISING MATCHBOX

Place an empty matchbox on the back of your hand. The drawer of the box should be slightly open as you do this.

As you set the box in place, position it so that the open drawer is on the fleshy part of the hand, where your fingers start.

While you are positioning the matchbox close the drawer so as to catch some of your flesh in it.

If you now close your fingers the matchbox will rise upwards. Relax your fingers and the matchbox will lie down again – just like magic!

QUICK KNOT

It is impossible to tie a knot in a length of rope without letting go of one of the ends of the rope.

You impart this fact to your audience and then prove the opposite by actually tying a knot in a piece of rope without letting go of either end.

All you have to do is lay the rope down on a table.

Now cross your arms and pick up one end of the rope in each hand.

Simply by uncrossing your arms a knot will form in the rope – and you didn't let go of the ends.

THE PENNY DROPS

Bend a match into a V-shape without breaking it, and place it on the top of an empty bottle.

Put a small coin, such as a penny, on top of the match. Now challenge anyone to get the penny into the bottle without touching the match, bottle, or coin and without shaking the table.

When your friends accept defeat, you show them how it is done.

All you have to do is dribble a few drops of water on to the centre of the V. This will cause the V to open and the coin will fall into the bottle.

BANANA SPLIT

A banana is peeled and the fruit inside is seen to be sliced into a number of pieces.

You can tell your audience that this is the latest invention – a ready-sliced banana.

In reality the banana is prepared well beforehand.

Push a needle into one of the banana 'seams'. Now work the needle back and forth inside the skin so it cuts the fruit.

Do this several more times at other points along the banana.

From the outside the banana looks quite ordinary, but when it is peeled the fruit will fall into pieces.

MAGNETIC PENCIL

In this trick you make a pencil adhere to your left hand.

You take the pencil in your left hand and grasp your left wrist with your right hand.

Then you open out your left hand, and the pencil remains sticking to it as if held in place with a magnet.

When you grasp your left wrist you secretly extend your right forefinger. It is this, not magnetism, which holds the pencil in position.

STICKY FINGERS

The effect of this trick is the same as the last one – a pencil seems to adhere to your hand by magic.

For this version you do not grasp your wrist; you grasp your forearm.

Anyone knowing the previous trick will be baffled by this one, for your finger is simply not long enough to reach the pencil. But you've fooled them again! A ruler tucked down your sleeve is what holds the pencil in place.

COIN STAND

A coin is balanced on the back of the hand.

Although not really a magic trick, this stunt is worth knowing as a useful lead-in to other tricks with coins.

The secret is a small pin held between the fingers.

Take the coin, with the pin hidden behind it, and place it upright on the back of your hand. At the same time, unbeknown to your audience, push the pin between your fingers. Grip the pin between your fingers and the coin will appear to be balancing upright.

Simply reverse the above movements to take the coin from the back of your hand.

If you want to use the coin for other tricks afterwards, allow the pin to drop unseen on to the floor leaving your hands empty.

BLOOD WILL TELL

A coin is handed to a spectator with the request that he hide the coin in either hand without letting you know which hand he chooses.

To convince the audience that everything is fair and above-board you turn your back so you cannot see which hand is chosen.

Now you ask the spectator to lift the hand concealing the coin up to his forehead and to concentrate as hard as he can.

After a short while, you ask him to lower his hand and you then turn round.

You can tell at once which hand is concealing the coin.

The title of this trick gives you a clue as to how it is done. When the spectator holds his hand up to his forehead, blood drains from it and it becomes paler than the other hand.

All you have to do is look at the spectator's hands. The paler one is the hand that conceals the coin.

QUICK CHANGE

You show a large Ace of Diamonds, on the other side of which is a Four of Diamonds. When the card is turned over, the Ace has changed to the Three of Diamonds. Turning the card over again reveals that the Four has now changed to the Six of Diamonds.

For this trick you will have to make a special card. On one side draw two diamond shapes, as shown. The other side has five diamonds on it.

Hold the 'two side' with the bottom diamond covered, and it looks like an Ace. Hold it with the blank space covered, and it appears to be a Three.

The same principle applies to the other side of the card. Hold it with the blank space covered, and it looks like a Six. Hold it with the diamond opposite the blank space covered, and it looks like a Four.

By changing your hand positions every time you turn the card over, it is possible to show an Ace, then a Four, followed by a Three, and then a Six.

ANTI-MAGNETIC STRAWS

'It is a well established fact that the like poles of magnets repel each other. But did you know that the same is true of drinking straws?'

As you say this, you place two drinking straws on the table in front of you.

Point to the space between the straws and explain that this is the source of the anti-magnetism. As you say this the straws start to roll apart. It looks as though what you said is true.

Don't believe a word of it! What really happens is that you pretend to concentrate on the point between the straws, but you are really gently blowing at it. It is this blowing, not anti-magnetism, that makes the straws roll apart.

CENTRE CARD

Glue five playing cards together. It is a good idea to have a distinctive card in the centre. For example, have four black cards with a red card in the middle.

Show these glued cards to a spectator and hand him a paper clip. Explain that all he has to do is place the clip on the Ace of Hearts (or whatever the central card happens to be), but that you are going to make the task a little more difficult by turning the cards over.

Turn the five cards face down and allow the spectator to attach the clip to the central card.

When this has been done, turn the cards face up again. To everyone's surprise the clip is nowhere near the central card!

This trick works automatically. But let the audience believe that you do it by difficult sleight of hand.

CRAWLING COIN

Place a 1p coin on a table, which must be covered with a table-cloth. On either side of this coin, place two 10p coins.

Next, place a glass tumbler on the two 10p coins, as shown.

Cover the tumbler with a handkerchief and say that you will get the 1p coin out from beneath the tumbler without touching the coins, the handkerchief, or the tumbler.

All you have to do is scratch the table-cloth a short distance away from the tumbler. In a little while the 1p coin will crawl out from beneath the tumbler towards you.

CASH TURNOVER

All you need for this trick is a currency note.

Follow the description and the pictures with a note in your hands.

Hold the note between the fingers and thumb of the left hand.

Fold the note in half lengthwise; bringing the top half down on to the lower portion.

Next fold the note in half the other way, but make sure that you fold it away from you.

Now fold the note in half again. This time fold it towards you.

You now unfold the note, opening all the folds from your side.

At the start of the sequence the note was the right way up, but when you finish it has turned upside down!

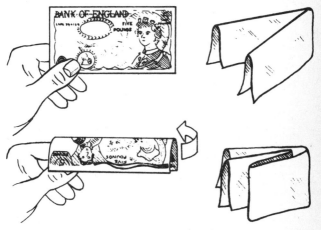

COIN DISCOVERY

For this trick you show a coin and three covers. The covers can be anything that will go over the coin – matchbox drawers, plastic cups, or even empty tin cans.

The coin is placed under any of the three covers, and then, while the performer is out of the room or his back is turned, a spectator moves the covers about as much as he fancies.

When the performer looks again he can identify which of the covers hides the coin.

Attached to the coin with a blob of glue is a fine hair which is long enough to stick out beyond the cover when it is over the coin. The covers may be moved about as much as anyone wishes. The hair will always tell you under which cover the coin is hidden.

CLIPPED

For this trick you need two paper-clips and a sheet of paper about the size of a five-pound note. You might even borrow a real fiver for the trick.

Fold over about a third of the paper and attach one of the clips over the folded section.

Fold the longest end of the paper back the other way and with the second clip attach together the part just folded and the central portion.

Pull the ends of the paper apart sharply, and the two paper-clips will leap off and into the air.

Ask someone to pick up the clips. They will receive quite a surprise, for the clips are now linked together!

Follow the illustrations to see how the clips are attached to the paper and you will discover that the trick works automatically.

NOW YOU ARE A MAGICIAN

DICE PREDICTION

You take a sheet of paper and write something on it. You do not show what you have written, but simply fold the paper in half and place it to one side in full view.

Two dice are placed into a large matchbox. You close the matchbox drawer and shake the box. Ask a spectator to push the drawer open and to total the number of spots visible on the top sides of the dice.

After he calls out this total you ask someone else to read what you wrote on the paper. It is the same number!

For this trick you will need a household-size matchbox and four dice. Glue two of the dice inside one end of the matchbox drawer. Remember the total of the spots showing on the tops of these dice for that is what you will write on the paper.

When you perform you show the other two dice and drop them into the empty end of the matchbox drawer. Shake the box and the dice will be heard rattling around. Now push the drawer open, so that only the two glued dice can be seen. Naturally, the number of spots that the spectator announces will be exactly the number you predicted.

CARD MATCH

The magician passes his hand over the face of a playing card whereupon the card changes into a matchbox.

This trick can be useful if you have been doing card tricks and wish to follow by doing something with matches.

The illustrations show virtually the whole trick.

One third of the playing card is glued to the top of the matchbox. It is a good idea to score lightly along the folds, as shown by the dotted lines.

Now fold the card entirely over the box and glue a matchbox label on to the back of the area of the card that covers the top of the box.

In performance, you show the card with one hand and, as you pass your other hand over it, you simply close the card around the box.

You must remember to keep your fingers on the side of the box, so that the card does not open after you have performed the trick.

JUMPING PENCIL

If you need to use a pencil for an effect, this is a neat little trick to make your performance more amusing.

Place a thin elastic band over the third finger of your right hand.

Form your hand into a loose fist with the elastic hanging inside.

Take a long pencil and push it down inside your fist. As you do so make sure that the end of the pencil pushes against the elastic band.

Tighten your fist to stop the pencil from jumping out before you are ready.

As soon as you release your grip the pencil will fly up into the air, like an arrow leaving a bow.

Be sure to hold your fist so that the back of your thumb faces the audience and prevents them from seeing the elastic band.

RISING MATCH

The next three tricks can be performed either as individual effects, or one after the other to make up an intriguing little magical routine.

In the first of the trio you push open a matchbox and a match rises mysteriously from the top of the box.

You have to prepare the box beforehand by making a small hole in the top of the outer case, as shown.

Close the box and push a match into the hole.

When you slide the drawer open the match will be pushed up out through the hole.

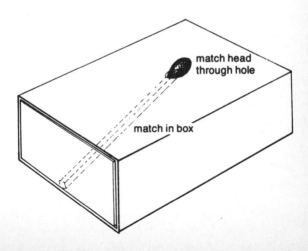

MATCH PENETRATION

A full box of matches is shown. It looks quite ordinary except for the fact that there is a hole in the top and bottom of the outer case.

There is a bit more secret preparation to do as well.

Cut a slit along the bottom of the drawer, as illustrated. You can conceal this slit by lining the bottom of the drawer with paper of the same colour as the interior of the drawer.

Put matches in the box, and you are ready to perform.

Open the box and remove a match, or make it rise up magically as described in 'Rising Match'.

Close the box and push the match down into the top hole, through the base of the drawer and out through the bottom hole.

Your audience will assume that the drawer cannot possibly move with a match pushed through it in this way. But, as a magician, you have no problem in doing the impossible. Simply push the drawer forward in the normal way.

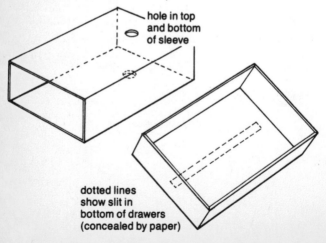

hole in top and bottom of sleeve

dotted lines show slit in bottom of drawers (concealed by paper)

BOX ESCAPE

A full matchbox is shown and the drawer taken out. The outer case is threaded on a length of ribbon, both ends of which are then held by spectators. The drawer is replaced and the box is covered with a handkerchief.

Despite the fact that both ends of the ribbon are held, you reach under the handkerchief and remove the matchbox from the ribbon by magic.

If you look at the illustration you will see the simple means used to achieve this effective trick.

Before your performance you secretly prise apart the two pieces of card that make up one side of the drawer.

Use a small blob of plasticine or wax to stick the sides back down again.

When you show the matchbox at the start of the trick it looks quite ordinary.

To remove the box from the ribbon you secretly open the side (under cover of the handkerchief), slip the ribbon out and press the sides together again.

If you study the last three tricks you will see that it is quite an easy matter to prepare one matchbox so it is suitable for all three which can then blend together into a short and intriguing interlude.

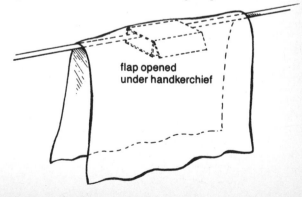

flap opened
under handkerchief

PENCIL PRODUCTION

Place a small pencil in the centre of a sheet of paper.

Fold the paper over the pencil, making sure that the upper length is longer than the lower, as shown in the second illustration. Leave the paper like this on your table until you are ready to show the trick.

Draw attention to the paper and then, starting at the fold, begin to roll it up. Keep rolling until the bottom (shorter) length comes over the top of the roll.

Now hold the right-hand edges down with your right hand and start to unroll the paper.

By the time you finish unrolling the pencil will have come into view.

PENNY ARCADE

For this trick you need a small coin (an English 1p coin is ideal – hence the title) and an empty matchbox.

During the performance the box must be held with the open side of the drawer downwards. It is a good idea, therefore, to mark the matchbox cover so that you know which way up it is.

Spin the coin on the table. Slam the matchbox down on the coin and ask, 'Will it be heads or tails?'

No matter what the answer, lift the box – and the coin has vanished.

What your audience do not realize is that you slammed the matchbox down with such force that the coin has penetrated the outer cover of the box and was thus forced into the drawer.

If you like you can open the matchbox (provided that you do not reveal the hole in its cover) to show the coin inside but it is generally considered a better tactic to put the matchbox to one side (with the coin still hidden inside) and to find the coin, a duplicate, of course, elsewhere.

BAFFLING BUS TICKETS

The principle used in 'Pencil Production', shown opposite can also be used to good effect with two bus tickets.

Borrow a friend's ticket and place it on top of yours. The upper end of the top ticket should be slightly above the end of your ticket

Start to roll the tickets together, beginning with the end nearest you.

Keep rolling until the far end of the bottom ticket flops over the roll.

Immediately unroll the tickets.

Your ticket is now on top and your friend's is underneath. They have changed places!

MOVE THE MATCHES

You take about ten matches from a matchbox and lay them in a row on the table.

Then you ask someone to transfer any number of matches, one at a time, from the right end of the row to the left.

Your back is turned while this action takes place, but as soon as you turn around again you are able to reveal exactly how many matches were moved.

The secret is so simple that many of you will hesitate to try it. But in the right hands it can appear to be a miracle, and, as many magicians will tell you, the simplest tricks are often the best.

Before your performance take one match, make a small pencil mark on each of its four sides, and then return it to the box.

Make sure your marked match is among those you remove from the box during your performance. When you lay out them in a row put the marked match at the extreme right.

Since the marked match is the first to be moved, it is easy to see how many altogether have changed places. All you have to do is count from the marked match to the left end of the row. It is as simple as that!

TRIPLE CHOICE

In this trick you locate three freely chosen cards that have been buried in the pack.

Before showing the trick you must do a little secret preparation. There is nothing difficult in this. All that is required is to put the four Kings on the top of the pack and the four Queens on the bottom. Place the pack back in its case and you are ready to baffle your audience.

When performance time comes take the cards from the case and spread them out, face down. Then invite someone to take any card from the centre of the pack.

Repeat this with two other spectators, so three cards have been freely chosen.

When the cards are being selected make sure that no one picks any of those cards you have planted at the top and bottom. Also be careful not to allow anyone to glimpse this secret arrangement.

Ask the spectators to show the rest of the audience their cards while you deal the pack into four face down piles.

Because of your advance preparation, the top card of each of the piles will be a Queen and the bottom cards will all be Kings but your spectators do not know this, of course.

Ask the first person to replace his card on top of any of the four piles. He is then to pick up any one of the remaining piles and place that on top of his card.

The second person is then invited to place his card on top of one of the three piles now on the table. He is then to pick up any other pile and place it on top of his card.

The third spectator is left with a choice of two piles. He is asked to place his card on either of them and then to put the remaining pile on top, so that the pack is complete once more.

Take the pack from the table and casually cut it several times, completing the cut each time. While you are doing this explain that the chosen cards are buried somewhere in this mixed-up pack and that no one could have any idea where they are.

Spread the cards, with their faces towards you, pick out three cards and place them face down on the table.

Ask the people to name their cards and turn the three cards over. They are the ones chosen earlier!

Because of the way you arranged the cards at the beginning, it is easy to find the chosen cards.

When you spread the cards out in front of you look for the Kings and Queens. Between each of three pairs, there will be a card; each one is one of the chosen cards.

RING RELEASE

A small ring is threaded on a length of string. Two spectators are each asked to hold one end of the string, with the ring hanging at the centre. A handkerchief is thrown over the ring.

The magician then places his hands beneath the handkerchief. After a few seconds he removes the handkerchief to show the ring still in position – but now secured by a match.

One of the spectators removes the match and the ring falls free of the string.

Apart from the string, handkerchief and match, you will need two identical rings for this trick.

One ring is hidden in the left hand and the other items are shown to the audience.

The visible ring is threaded on the string, the ends of which are held by two spectators. The ring on the string is then covered with the handkerchief.

Secretly pick up the match and then place both hands beneath the handkerchief. It is now quite easy to take the hidden ring and attach it to the string, using the match, as shown in the illustration.

Put your left hand over the previously threaded ring and then remove the handkerchief.

Run your left hand (with threaded ring concealed) along the string to the person on your left, as you ask him to remove the match. To do this he has to let go of the string and this allows you to take your left hand (still holding the concealed ring) off the left end of the string.

While the spectator is removing the central ring from the match, you have plenty of time to drop the other ring into your pocket and no one will be any the wiser as to how the trick was done.

COME TOGETHER KINGS

Remove the four Kings from the pack and show them to your audience. This appears to be straight-forward but you have secretly added two extra cards behind the second King, as shown in the illustration.

Close the fan of cards and place them on top of the pack.

Take the top card (a King) and place it at the bottom of the pack.

The next card, which the spectators think is a King but which is really one of the extra cards, is pushed into the centre of the pack.

The third card (which is also one of the extra cards) is pushed into the pack in the same way.

Finally the last card (really the second King) is shown and then placed back on the top of the pack.

Your audience should believe that the four Kings have been evenly distributed though the pack.

Cut the cards and complete the cut. If you wish, you can cut several more times, provided that you complete each cut.

Remind your audience that the Kings are separated from each other in the pack. Now spread the cards face up across the table. Point to the Kings: they have all come together!

How did you do it? Well, if you follow the instructions exactly, you will find that it works automatically.

PIN PUZZLE

For this trick you will need a large safety pin – at least 5 cm (2″) long – and a handkerchief.

Push the pin in and back out of the handkerchief and close it. Now hold the hinge part of the pin. The point should be facing upwards and held flat against the material.

Hold the material taut against the pin with the left hand as the right hand gives the pin a sharp tug to the right. The head of the pin runs along the handkerchief without tearing it.

In actual fact the material runs between the point and the head of the pin.

At the end of the run, the pin should be pushed forward to get the point back through the material. Most tricks require practice and that is certainly true of this one – especially if you want to do it with a borrowed handkerchief – for it requires a certain knack to manage it without tearing the material.

ANTI-GRAVITY MATCHES

A matchbox is opened to show it is full of matches. The drawer is then closed and the box turned upside down. Now the drawer is removed completely. Everyone will expect all the matches to fall out. But nothing happens – until you give the word of command, when the matches drop out on to the table.

The trick is accomplished by a piece of a matchstick jammed across the drawer, as shown.

Put the matches in the drawer, place the broken match in position and then push the drawer back into the box. The drawer can be opened about half-way to show the matches, without revealing the wedged half match.

Push the drawer back in and turn the box over.

Push the drawer out, but hold it on either side with finger and thumb to keep the broken match in position. The matches will not fall out.

Now say the magic word and release your grip on the drawer sides. All the matches will fall on to the table. The broken match will be hidden by all the others, so there is no clue as to how you achieved this remarkable feat.

A CALCULATED DISCOVERY

A pack of cards is well shuffled and about half of them are cut off to be used in this trick.

You then count these cards, face up, on to the table. Ask someone to make a mental note of any one of the cards dealt and at which number it falls. All you have to do is remember the first card dealt.

When you have gone through all the cards, turn them face down in your hands. Mention that some of the audience may be thinking the trick is going to be done not by magic but by arithmetic. To allay their suspicions, you ask someone to take several cards from the discarded portion of the pack and add them to the top of the packet you hold. It is obvious that no one could know the number of cards added at this point.

Have the packet cut several times so the cards are really mixed up.

Start looking through the cards searching for the first one dealt. While you are doing this, ask the first spectator for the position of the card he noted.

When you reach your 'key' card – the one you memorized at the beginning of the trick – start counting (to yourself) until you reach the number the spectator has just given you. That card will be the one he chose.

Ignore the fact that you now know the chosen card and continue to look through the rest of the cards.

Put them all aside and ask the spectator to think of his card. You then reveal its identity, as if you had read his mind.

A QUICK VANISH

A coin is shown between the thumb and forefinger of the left hand and then covered with a handkerchief. The right hand draws the handkerchief back towards the magician until the coin becomes visible again.

This action is repeated several times, but on the last time the coin disappears. There is nothing in the handkerchief, and the magician's hands are empty!

You will need to wear a jacket with a top pocket for this trick. Hold a coin between your left forefinger and thumb and cover it with a handkerchief.

With the right hand, take the corner of the handkerchief hanging down nearest you, and pull it towards you. If you pull slightly to the left, your right hand will come fairly near to your top pocket.

Now go through the actions again, but as you take the handkerchief this time, grip the coin (through the handkerchief) between the first and second fingers of your right hand. When your right hand is above your top pocket, drop the coin into it.

That is all there is to it. You will need to practise to get the actions smooth. To the audience, it will appear that you covered the coin a couple of times and that it then vanished.

Make a great play of showing the handkerchief on both sides afterwards to prove that the coin really has disappeared.

THINK OF A NUMBER

Say to a friend, 'Think of any number from one to sixty. Now divide it by three and tell me what remainder you have, if there is one.'

When your friend has done that you say, 'Now divide your chosen number by four and tell me what the remainder is.'

Then you say, 'Now I would like you to divide your chosen number by five and tell me what the remainder is, if any.'

You now tell him what number he chose.

In your head you take the first remainder and multiply it by 40, the second remainder is multiplied by 45, and the third by 36. Now add all three totals together. Divide the total by 60 and the remainder is the person's number. At first sight this may sound quite complicated but it is not too difficult. Here is an example to show you how it works:

If the chosen number is 47, the first division by three equals 15 with a remainder of two.

Divided by four this gives 11 with a remainder of three.

And when divided by five, the remainder is two.

Remainder one (2) muliplied by 40 gives 80.

Remainder two (3) multiplied by 45 gives 135.

Remainder three (2) multiplied by 36 gives 72.

Add these totals together (80 + 135 + 72) and you get 287. Divide this by 60, and it comes to four with a remainder of 47. The remainder is the only thing you are interested in, for that is the number originally thought of.

MENTAL FOURSOME

A pack of cards is shuffled and cut into four piles.

Using your uncanny mental ability, you can name the top card of each of the four piles.

How do you do it? Simple, that's how!

Have the cards shuffled by a spectator and returned to you. You then pass them to a second spectator; but as you do so you push the top card slightly to one side so that you can glimpse it.

Remember this card.

Ask the second spectator to cut the pack into four piles.

Remember which pile has the original top card – the one you glimpsed.

Let us assume that it was the Six of Diamonds.

Announce that you are going to try to name the top card on each of the piles.

Say, 'Six of Diamonds', but remove the top card from one of the other three piles.

Look at this card, but do not show it to anyone. Let us assume that this is the Four of Clubs.

You now announce that the next card will be the Four of Clubs. Take the top card from one of the other piles but do not show its face. We will assume that this is the Jack of Spades.

Call 'Jack of Spades', and take a card from the top of the third pile. Let's say that this is the King of Hearts.

Now touch the last pile (the one that you know has the Six of Diamonds on top) and say, 'King of Hearts'.

Lift off the top card and place it below the three you hold in your hand.

Now show the four cards you hold. They are the ones you have just named!

All through this trick you stay one step ahead of your audience. You must act convincingly to make it effective.

BROKEN AND RESTORED MATCH

A match is placed inside a handkerchief and then broken. Someone from the audience can do this, to make sure that the match really is broken in two.

You then shake the match from the handkerchief – and it is completely restored!

To convince everyone that there is only one match, you ask a spectator to mark it with a pencil before the start of the trick.

In spite of this precaution of marking the match two matches are indeed used, but the audience sees only one.

The second match is concealed inside the hem of the handkerchief.

When the first match is placed inside the handkerchief you allow the spectator to break the one hidden in the hem.

Thus the first match can be dropped from the handkerchief apparently restored, because it was never broken in the first place!

COLOUR LOCATION

Before showing this trick, secretly separate a pack of cards into red cards and black. Put the pack back together so that all the red cards are in the top half.

When someone asks you to do a trick, spread the cards out face down. Only spread out the top (red) half of the pack.

Ask the spectator to take a card, remember it, and then return it to the pack. For this replacement, you spread out only the bottom (black) half of the pack.

Cut the pack a few times, completing the cut each time. Spread the cards with their faces towards you and somewhere among the black cards you will see a solitary red one. That is the chosen card. Take it from the pack and ask for the name of the selected card. Then show the card you hold, as you take your well deserved applause.

MULTIPLYING MONEY

You show three coins and count them from your hand on to a small tray. Everyone can see there are only three coins and that your hands are empty.

The coins are then tipped from the tray into your hand. Without any hesitation, you open your hand. There are now seven coins; four extra coins have appeared in your hand by magic.

You will need to make a special tray.

This requires three sheets of cardboard, each measuring about 20 cm by 10 (8″ × 4″). The actual size is not important, provided that you can hold the tray without fumbling.

Take one sheet of card and cut a long slot in it, as shown. It must be wide enough and long enough to take the coins you intend to use.

Glue the other pieces of cardboard to each side of this special card so that you end up with a flat card in which there is a hidden cavity.

Put four coins in this cavity and you are ready to perform the trick.

Show three coins and count them one by one on to the top of the cardboard tray.

Let eveyone see that your hands are empty. Now tip the coins from the tray. At the same time, the hidden coins slide from the cavity into your waiting hand.

The spectators believe that you still have only three coins in your hand.

Put the tray to one side and open your hand to reveal that you actually hold seven coins.

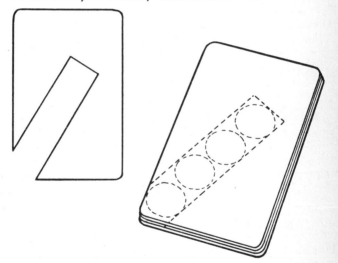

ONE OF FOUR

Have a pack of cards shuffled and remove four cards. Show these to a spectator and ask him to think of any one of them, but not to tell you which it is. Put the cards on the table.

Now remove a further four, and show them to a second spectator with the same request. He, too, is to remember just one card.

Put these four on top of the first four.

Repeat these actions with two more spectators, so that you have four cards being remembered, and a pile of sixteen on the table.

Deal out the cards into four piles of four cards each.

Show the cards in each pile in turn to the first spectator and ask him to indicate which pile contains his card.

Whichever pile he indicates his card will be the first in that pile. Do the same with the second spectator and his card will be the second in the indicated pile.

The third spectator's card will be the third in the pile he indicates, and the fourth spectator's card will be the fourth in the pile he indicates.

It may be that more than one spectator will indicate the same pile. Do not worry about this, for the rule still holds true: the first spectator's card will be in the first position; the second spectator's card will be in the second position; the third will be in the third place; and the fourth will be in the fourth position.

All you now have to do is to pretend to read the minds of your spectators and announce the name of each chosen card.

THE TWENTY-FIVE CARD TRICK

From a shuffled pack deal out twenty-five cards face up in five rows of five cards.

Ask someone to think of any one of the cards shown and tell you in which row it is.

Make a mental note of the card at the left end of that row. This is your 'key' card.

Pick up the cards, beginning with the one at the far right of the bottom row. Place it on the card immediately above it in the next row. Keep working upward in this way, each time placing all the cards you hold on top of the next card above.

When you reach the top of the line of cards on the far right; start at the bottom of the next line, again collecting cards as you move upward.

Repeat this with every line, until you have picked up all the cards.

Now deal them out into five horizontal rows again.

Look for your 'key' card as you ask the spectator in which row his card now appears.

His card will be in the same vertical line as the 'key', and, since he tells you the row, you can immediately identify it.

RING ON

A long piece of rope is tied to one of the magician's wrists. The other end is tied to the other wrist.

A plastic ring, or bangle, is then shown and examined.

The magician takes the ring and turns his back for a second. When he turns round, the ring is seen to be threaded on the rope.

What the audience do not realize is that two identical rings are used.

Before showing the trick, put one of the rings on your left arm and cover it with your sleeve.

Show the rope; have it tied to your wrists, and then show the ring.

Take the ring and turn your back. As soon as your back is turned put the ring you have shown to your audience into an inside pocket; now pull the duplicate ring down from your sleeve and on to the rope. This will require some practice to ensure success.

Turn back to face your audience, and take your applause.

COIN IN HANDKERCHIEF

This is a useful way to make a coin vanish for it needs no apparatus other than the coin and a handkerchief.

Place the handkerchief flat on the table and put the coin in its centre, as in the first illustration (a).

Fold the handkerchief up over the coin so it forms a triangular shape (b).

Now take the corner on the left and fold it over to the right (c).

Once again, fold the handkerchief in half (d) and then lift it up from the table with the coin inside.

Look at the right corner of the handkerchief and you will see that it is made up of four points. Two are nested together and the other two are separate.

Take the two separate points, one in each hand and pull your hands apart sharply.

With the handkerchief stretched between your hands it looks as though the coin has vanished. But it is actually hidden in a fold along the crease of the handkerchief (e).

With practice you can tilt your hands so that the coin will roll unseen along the fold and into one hand. Keep the coin hidden in your hand as you shake out the handkerchief: the coin has disappeared completely!

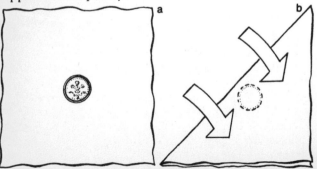

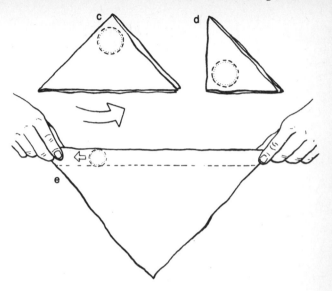

SPOT ON

A pack of cards is shuffled, then handed to one of your audience.

He is invited to take any three cards from the pack and place them on the table.

Taking the number of spots on each card as a starting point he has to put enough cards on top of each card to make every pile total fifteen.

If, for example, one card is the Eight of Clubs, he must add seven cards to reach fifteen. If the card is a Two, then thirteen cards have to be added. A Six will require the addition of nine cards.

In this trick, an Ace counts as eleven and the picture cards as ten.

When the spectator has counted out all the cards required he hands the rest of the pack back to you. Within seconds you can tell your audience the total number of pips on the three selected cards.

You have to prepare the pack in advance by removing the Two's, Three's, Four's, Five's and Six's.

With the 32 cards remaining you are ready to perform.

Go through the routine as explained above. When what is left of the pack is handed back to you quickly count the cards and then add sixteen to your total. The result will be the total of the spots on the three selected cards.

Let us take a look at an example:

Assume that the three selected cards are a Nine, a Seven and a Jack.

On the first card, the spectator will place six cards to bring the total to fifteen. On the second, he will put eight cards, and on the Jack (which counts as ten, remember) he will place five cards.

This leaves just ten cards. Add sixteen and you arrive at a total of twenty-six. Counting picture cards as ten, the three cards (Jack, Nine and Seven) add up to twenty-six!

PIN PENETRATION

Two safety pins are linked together. You blow on them and they separate without being opened.

In fact the pins do open and close to achieve this effect, but it happens so fast that no one sees it.

You will need two large safety pins which you link together. Hold them at the hinges, between fingers and thumbs, as shown in the illustration.

Make sure that the point of the pin on the left is uppermost and that of the pin on the right is lower.

Now pull the pins apart, but as you do so pull the right pin slightly faster and in a downwards direction.

It takes practice to get the movements correct, but they are not difficult. The right pin actually pulls the left one open a fraction; it moves between the point and the head, and the left pin then closes. But do not tell the spectators that. Let them believe that you caused solid to penetrate solid!

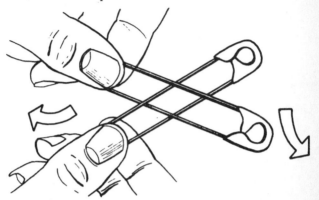

COLOURED THOUGHTS

Place a box of coloured crayons on your table.

Ask someone to remove one of the crayons from the box while your back is turned.

Now ask that the selected crayon be handed to you behind your back, and that the remaining crayons be removed from sight.

Turn round to face the audience. After a few moments' concentration, you reveal the colour of the chosen crayon.

All you need for this trick is the box of crayons and the normal acting ability required for all conjuring effects.

After the crayon has been handed to you, turn round to face the audience, still holding the crayon behind your back.

Unbeknown to your spectators, you secretly dig your right thumb-nail into the crayon.

With the crayon still behind your back, bring your

right hand forward and point to the spectator who chose the crayon. Say, 'I just want you to concentrate on the colour you chose.'

As you say this, take a quick glance at your thumb-nail. It tells you all you need to know!

TRAVELLING COIN

A coin is placed on the palm of each hand and the hands are turned over on to the table top.

Ask someone how many coins are under each hand. He will naturally reply that there is one under each.

You then lift your hands. There are now two coins under your left hand and nothing beneath your right. A coin has travelled invisibly from one hand to the other. This trick will give you the reputation of being able to perform difficult sleight of hand. But it is really quite easy.

Put one coin on the palm of your left hand. The second coin is placed at the base of the first and second fingers of the right hand. The positioning of the coins is important.

Place your hands on the table, palms uppermost. They should be about 25 cm (10″) apart.

Without raising your hands from the table, turn them both over and inwards. Because of the positioning of the coins, the one on the right hand will be thrown across to the left, where it is caught as the hand turns over on to the table top.

This movement happens so quickly that it is impossible to see.

Lift your hands to show that the coin has travelled from right to left.

If you are left-handed you may find that the trick works better if the position of the coins is reversed, so that the one from the left hand is thrown to the right.

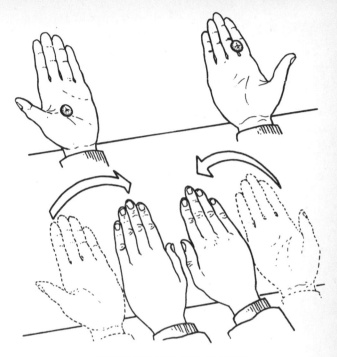

PENETRATING BAND

Hold your right hand with the back of it facing the audience.

Take an elastic band and place it over the first and second fingers of your right hand.

With your left hand, stretch the band to show it is really is over your right fingers. As you release the band clench your right hand into a fist so that the third and fourth fingers go into the band.

Your audience should not be aware of this. To them, it must appear that the band was simply stretched and then released.

You, of course, can see that the band is over all your fingers, but to the audience it looks as though it is still over only the first two.

All you now have to do is to open your hand quickly. The band jumps from the first two fingers and is now over the third and fourth!

If you wish, you can now make the band return to the first two fingers. To do this you simply repeat the stretching action and close your fist to get all four fingers back in the band again. When you open your hand this time, the band will jump back to the first two fingers.

IMPOSSIBLE RELEASE

For this effect you will need two large scarves and about two metres (two yards) of soft rope.

Ask someone to tie your wrists together with one of the scarves. Keep your fists closed while this is being done.

Meanwhile, a second spectator has been examining the rope to make sure it is strong and that there is nothing unusual about it.

Ask the second spectator to pass the rope between your wrists, as shown in the first picture (a).

Someone holds both ends of the rope, and the second scarf is thrown over your wrists.

Within a short time, you have managed to free yourself from the rope without undoing the scarf around your wrists.

To do this, you open your hands and pull backwards slightly. This movement brings the rope hard against the scarf so that you can trap the centre of the rope between the heels of your hands (b).

Now step towards the person holding the rope, which slackens it, then work your hands backwards and forwards manoeuvring the rope up towards your palms.

Keep doing this until your hands are in a position where you can bend the right hand inwards and slip your fingers into the loop of rope (c).

Slip the whole of your hand through the loop, and step backwards, thus pulling the rope taut again.

Ask the person holding the rope to pull, and the rope will be drawn beneath the scarf and come free.

Immediately clench your fists as before, and toss the covering scarf into the air as dramatically as you can.

Your wrists are still securely tied, but you are free of the rope!

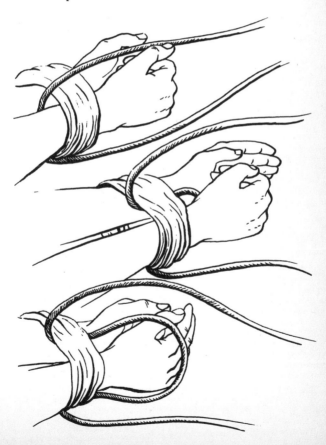

THE TWENTY-ONE CARD TRICK

Remove twenty-one cards from a pack, shuffle them and then deal them out into three equal piles.

Show each group of cards in turn to a spectator, asking him to think of any one of the cards.

Then ask him which of the three groups contains his card. Place that group between the other two.

Once again deal out the twenty-one cards into three equal piles. Show the spectator the cards of each pile in turn, and ask which one contains the chosen card.

Put the pile with that card between the other two as before and deal into three piles again.

Again spread the cards, asking the spectator to indicate which pile contains his card.

Believe it or not but you now know what card the spectator has in mind. It is the middle one in the last group he has indicated.

To reveal which card it is you can take a quick glance at the central card and then, by pretending to read the spectator's mind, call out its name. Alternatively, you can reassemble all the cards (again placing the selected group between the other two) and count down to the eleventh card which is the one the spectator chose.

INDESTRUCTIBLE STRING

A thin string is threaded through a drinking straw. The centre portion of the straw is cut away but the string remains in one piece.

Unbeknown to the audience the straw has a 1 cm (0.4″) long cut at the centre.

When the straw is bent, the string goes through the slit, as shown. This is concealed by the hand holding the straw.

The straw can now be cut across the folded portion.

The two remaining pieces of straw are held in the left hand while the right hand pulls out the string, which is intact.

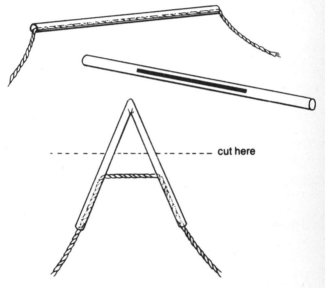

cut here

MATCHBOX PENCIL-CASE

Only a magician would carry a pencil in a matchbox – especially if the pencil is some five times longer than the box that contains it!

The effect of this trick is that you open a matchbox and pull a long pencil from it. The longer the pencil, the more effective the trick.

To prepare for this trick you cut one end off the drawer of a matchbox. Tuck the pencil down your right sleeve and you are ready to perform.

Remove the matchbox from your pocket and hold it in your right hand. You must keep the open end as near to the end of the pencil as possible.

Open the matchbox, being careful, of course, not to reveal the open end.

As you do this, flex your right hand inwards towards the wrist a little, so that the pencil begins to enter the open end of the box.

With your left hand reach into the drawer of the box, grasp the tip of the pencil, and pull it out.

The back of your right hand conceals the way the pencil gets into the box.

CARD LOCATION

It is always useful to be able to locate a playing card chosen by a spectator, for it is a trick that most of your audience will expect you to know how to do as elementary magic.

There are several ways to do it but this is one of the simplest and, therefore, one of the most effective.

Have a pack of cards shuffled by a spectator. Take the cards back and then place them on the table. In doing this, tilt the cards slightly so that you can get a glimpse of the bottom card. Do this casually: no one must suspect what you are up to.

Ask a spectator to lift off some of the cards; take out the one at that place in the pack, and then put back the cut-off portion.

Now ask the spectator to look at his chosen card and show it to the rest of the audience. This is a useful thing to do in any card trick, just in case the person forgets the card in question.

The spectator puts his card on top of the pack. You then cut the pack and complete the cut. You now take the pack and run through it only once, with the cards facing you. You immediately name the chosen card.

How do you know? Well, if you follow the above instructions correctly, the chosen card will always be to the right of the card you noted earlier.

DISSOLVING COIN

In this trick a coin vanishes when it is dropped into a glass of water.

You will need, in addition to the coin and the glass of water, a handkerchief and a glass disc the size of the coin you intend to use.

Place the glass of water, the handkerchief and the coin on your table. Conceal the glass disc in your hand – and you are ready to perform.

Keeping the disc concealed, pick up the coin and cover it with the handkerchief. Under cover of the handkerchief exchange the coin for the disc and then ask someone to hold it through the material. This gives you ample opportunity to remove your hand and secretly drop the coin into a pocket.

Ask the person who is holding what he thinks is the coin to lift it above the glass of water and then let go. Everyone will hear the splash of what they believe to be the coin as it drops into the water.

The handkerchief is removed and shown to be empty. Since the glass disc cannot be seen, the glass of water appears to be empty. The coin has dissolved!

FIND THE LADY

'Find the Lady' is a classic trick normally accomplished by well practised sleight of hand. This is an easier version, but just as effective.

You will need to make a special card like the one shown overleaf. This is simply a Two of Clubs with part of a Queen of Hearts glued to it.

In addition to this special card, you will need a Joker and a Three of Clubs.

Assemble the cards as shown in the second picture, making certain that the Joker is completely hidden behind the Three of Clubs.

Show the cards to your audience and draw

attention to the fact that there is a red Queen between the two black cards.

Turn the fan of cards over, spreading the two front cards (the Three and the secret Joker) apart as you do so.

Ask someone to pull out the Queen. Naturally he will take the centre card.

When he turns over what he thought was the Queen, he will be astonished to find that he has ended up with the Joker!

TELEPHONE TELEPATHY

A card is chosen by a member of the audience. He speaks to a friend of yours on the telephone, and your friend reveals the name of the card, even though he may be several miles away.

When the card has been selected, ask for it to be shown to everyone in the room. Make sure that you see it as well.

You now say that you are going to telephone your friend, who has an amazing ability. Your friend will, of course, have been forewarned that you would ring at a certain time.

When he answers the telephone, he names the four card suits slowly: 'Clubs . . . Hearts . . . Spades . . . Diamonds.' As soon as he mentions the suit of the chosen card you say, 'Hello, is Fred Blogs (your friend's name) there?' He now knows the correct suit.

He then starts counting through the card values, slowly: 'Ace, two, three, four . . .'

This time you stop him at the right number by saying something like 'Hello, Fred. I have a call for you.'

He now knows both the value and the suit of the card.

Hand the telephone to the spectator who chose the card and your mind-reading friend tells him which one it was.

THE ESCAPING WASHERS

Show your audience five or six metal washers and a piece of string.

Fold the string in half and push its centre through one of the washers. Now take the ends of the string and push them through the string loop on the far side of the washer – the side away from you. This knots the washer to the string, as shown in the illustration (a) overleaf.

Thread the two ends of the string through the remaining washers so that they are positioned as in the second picture (b).

Ask two spectators each to hold one end of the string. Then you toss a large handkerchief over the washers.

Point out that it is impossible for the washers to

be released while the ends of the string are being held.

Place your hands beneath the handkerchief and pull the loop down over the bottom washer. The third illustration (c) shows this movement in progress.

This action frees the bottom washer – and all the others will slide off the string.

Whisk the handkerchief away, and allow the washers to pour from your hand and on to the table.

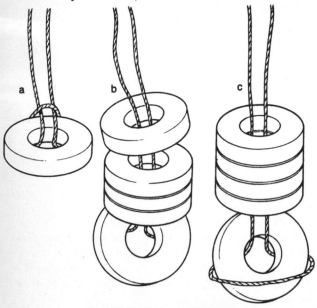

RING OF DECEPTION

For this trick you will need a large sheet of paper; a smaller piece of the same paper; a plastic ring about five centimetres (two inches) in diameter, and a sheet of cardboard large enough to cover the ring.

Glue the small piece of paper to the ring and then trim off the excess.

Place the large sheet on the table. Put the ring, paper side down, on top of the sheet and have the cardboard nearby. You are now ready to show a baffling feat of magic.

Borrow a coin and place it on the sheet. Pick up the cardboard and the ring together, with the ring underneath. Drop them on top of the coin.

Pause for a second or two and then lift the cardboard. It appears that the coin has vanished.

Thanks to the secret paper attached to the ring, the audience think that what they see through the ring is the large sheet of paper. Replace the cardboard on top of the ring.

Now lift both cardboard and ring together – and the coin reappears!

CARD LEAP

A card is chosen by a spectator and replaced in the pack.

When you give the word of command, the selected card leaps from the pack.

To do this trick, you will need a pack of cards, two additional cards, an elastic band and a pair of scissors.

First cut a slit halfway down each of the two extra cards as shown overleaf. Cut about five centimetres (two inches) from the elastic band and slide each of the two ends into the slits in the cards. Tie a knot at each end of the band to stop it being pulled through the slit.

Place these joined cards in the pack and you are ready.

Spread out the cards and ask someone to select one, making sure that he does not take the joined cards.

Ask him to remember his card and return it to the pack. You open the pack to help in this action and, unbeknown to the audience, you open it between the joined cards.

As the chosen card is pushed home, it presses against the elastic band. So you must hold the pack quite firmly, to prevent the card from leaping out of the pack too soon.

After a suitably short interval, raise the pack and ask the spectator to name his card. As soon as he does you slacken your grip on the pack and the secret elastic band will catapult the card into the air.

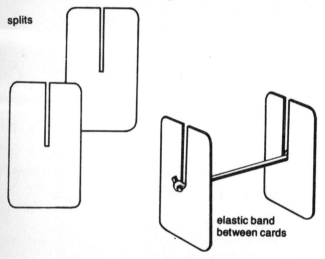

splits

elastic band
between cards

GLASS THROUGH TABLE

This a good trick to perform at a party when you are seated at a table.

To the audience, it appears that you place a glass under the table-cloth and then smash it right through the table-top.

All you need is a disc of thin cardboard about the same diameter as an ordinary glass tumbler. Keep the disc in your pocket until you want to show the trick.

When no one is looking, take the disc secretly from your pocket and rest it on one of your knees.

Now offer to show everyone your latest miracle. Allow both your hands to be seen empty as you speak, but do not make any mention of this fact.

Your left hand now goes down behind the table to lift the table cloth. On its downward journey, you take the cardboard disc from your knee. Lift the cloth with the same hand, and slide the disc under the cloth.

Take a glass tumbler in your right hand and appear to place it under the cloth.

What you really do is place the glass between your knees. Bring your empty right hand up above the table and grasp the cardboard disc through the cloth. It looks as if you are holding the glass.

Suddenly bang the disc down flat on the table.

Wait just a second for the impact to register. Then reach under the table; retrieve the glass from between your knees, and bring it back up into view.

If you act out this charade convincingly, your friends will believe you really did manage to pass an ordinary glass through a solid table.

MONEY MAGIC

For this feat you will need to solder a small loop of wire to a coin.

With this little gadget you can perform a wide variety of magical movements that appear to be well practised sleight of hand.

Since everyone's hands are different, it is a good idea to experiment with this piece of apparatus to discover what movements are best for you.

Here is one you can try immediately:

Hook the wire on to your second finger so that the coin hangs against your palm.

Turn your hand over, and at the same time push

the coin between the first and second fingers so that it now hangs at the back of your hand.

If you start with the back of your hand facing your audience, it appears that you have shown both sides of your hand empty. You can then, with a slight upward and forward movement of your hand, catch the coin at your fingertips.

A reversal of these movements will enable you to make a coin vanish just as easily.

Practise with this looped coin and you will soon come up with other actions that will prove equally baffling to your audience.

SLEIGHT OF FOOT

Show a coin and toss it in the air a few times. On the last throw, pretend to fumble the catch and allow the coin to fall to the floor.

As you move forward to pick it up, position your right foot so that it is just behind the coin.

Bend down to pick up the coin. Place your fingers on its furthest edge and flick it towards your foot. Lift your toe upwards at the same time, and the coin will go under it.

Put your toe back down immediately. Do this as you begin to straighten up. Keep your hand clasped, as if holding the coin.

It should all be one continuous movement – to look as if you have simply bent down and picked up the coin.

As with all magic, the success of this trick depends upon your acting ability. And there is more acting to come if you are to succeed in fooling the spectators.

Still holding the imaginary coin, raise your right hand and pretend to place the coin into the left hand.

After a suitable pause, slowly open your left hand – the coin has vanished!

JUST FOR YOU

A coin vanishes from your hands. It is obvious that your hands are completely empty and the person watching has no idea where the coin has gone.

Unfortunately this can be performed for only one person, since anyone else watching will see how the trick is done. It is, however, still worth learning for the times when you want to perform a trick for just one person.

Have your friend stand facing you with his right hand outstretched.

Show a coin and explain that your are going to touch it against his hand three times. The third time, he is to take the coin from you as quickly as possible.

Emphasize that he must keep his eyes on his own hand to ensure proper concentration.

Touch his palm with the coin. Count 'One'. Immediately bring the hand holding the coin up to the top of your head, then back down again to touch your friend's palm as you say, 'Two'.

Move your hand again up to your head. Without pausing, place the coin on top of your head. Still pretending to hold the coin, bring your hand down and touch your friend's palm as you say, 'Three'.

Your friend closes his hand in an attempt to grab the coin. You show your hands empty, and ask him to open his. The coin has vanished!

CAUGHT!

This is an effective way to reveal a chosen card.

Have a card chosen and find out its identity, as described on page 50. Go through the cards and move the selected one to the bottom of the pack.

Pretend to cough; bring your hand up to your mouth, and secretly lick your thumb.

Hold the pack in your hand with your moistened thumb against the bottom (selected) card.

Throw the whole pack up in the air and lunge forward with your hand.

The selected card will remain stuck to your thumb, but it will look as though you have plucked just one card from the shower of cards.

Show the card you hold. Abracadabra! It is the selected card!

VANISHING COIN

This is a useful way to make a coin disappear before the eyes of your spectators.

Take a coin between the thumb and forefinger of your left hand, as shown in the first illustration opposite (a).

Bring the right hand over the coin, but make sure that the right thumb goes beneath the coin, as shown (b).

Close the right hand as if to take the coin. You really allow the coin to drop from your left fingers into the left hand (c). The right hand continues to close and then moves off to the right as if holding the coin (d).

Timing, smoothness of action and practice are essential for the successful accomplishment of this deceit.

Continue to act as if the coin is in your right hand. Look at this hand and really concentrate on it – and the attention of your audience will be directed towards it.

Since everyone's attention is on the right hand, you have ample opportunity to drop the coin from your left hand into a pocket.

Now blow on the right hand, to call attention to it – and then open it slowly to show that the coin has vanished.

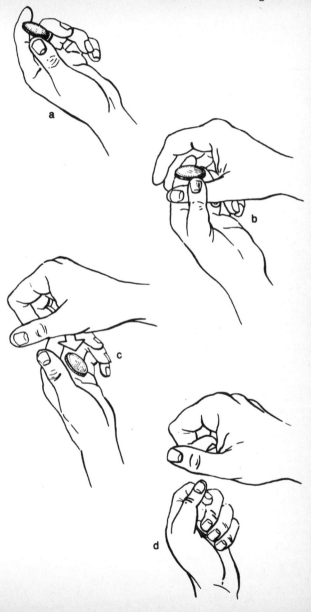

SPLIT IN TWO

In this trick you borrow a £10 note and magically change it into two £5 notes.

It requires a bit of work beforehand but once made it will last for a number of performances.

You will need five pieces of fairly stiff paper. The first sheet should be about 15 cm (6") square; the next two sheets are each about 12.5 cm (5") square; and the last two sheets are each 9 cm (3.5") square.

Fold each sheet of paper into a packet, as shown.

Glue the two medium sized packets (the 12.5 cm/ 5" sheets) back to back. The result should look like just one packet, but you can open it from either side. This is the main secret of the trick.

Fold two £5 notes together and place them inside one of the smallest packets. Put this packet in one side of your special double packet. The second – empty – small packet is placed in the other side of the double one.

Unfold the large sheet and place the double packet in its centre. It must be placed so that the empty small packet will be on top when it is opened. Close up the large sheet and you are ready to show the trick – after you have practised it thoroughly.

At the start of the trick you open the three packets and ask for the loan of a £10 note. Fold the note and place it in the small packet, which is then folded inside the middle (double) packet.

Place the middle packet on to the centre of the large sheet, but secretly turn it over as you do so.

Close the large packet and announce that you are going to make the £10 note disappear.

Make a few magic incantations and open the three packets one at a time. When the third packet is opened to reveal the two £5 notes, express disappointment that the trick has gone wrong. The audience will realize that the £10 note has changed into two £5 notes but you pretend not to notice this.

Fold the £5 notes again and wrap the whole lot up as before – once again secretly turning the middle packet over in the process.

Say you will have one more go at making the £10 vanish.

Open the packets once again – this time to reveal the £10 note. Hand it back to its owner with some comment that every magician has a trick go wrong sometimes.

One of the nice aspects of this trick is that you have performed some magic without your apparent knowledge.

You can, if you wish, perform this trick as a straightforward transformation of one £10 note into two £5 notes – which you return to the person who lent you the £10.

SECRETS OF THE PROFESSIONALS

CIRCLES OF MYSTERY

A loop of paper is cut along the centre, and it produces two loops, as one would expect.

But there is quite a surprise when two similar loops are cut in the same way.

The second loop becomes two loops – but they are linked together. And the third loop transforms itself into one large loop, twice the size of the original!

All you need are a pair of scissors and three loops of paper. The loops, however, are prepared in a special way.

The first one is simply a strip of paper with the two ends glued together.

The second is made in the same way, but one end of the strip is given a half turn before the two ends are glued together.

The third strip is given a complete turn before the ends are glued.

From now on everything works automatically. Cut each loop along the centre and the first will produce two loops, the second two loops linked together and the third one large loop.

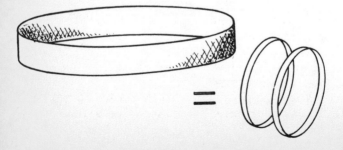

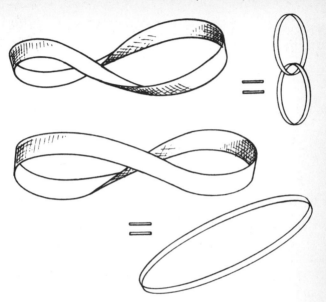

ROLL UP, ROLL UP

A large sheet of cartridge paper – about 30 x 40 cm (12" x 16") – is rolled into a tube. You then produce ribbons from the tube.

To accomplish this trick you must do some work beforehand.

Fold your sheet of cartridge (or other stiff) paper in half.

Roll the folded paper into a tube and hold it in shape with two elastic bands. Leave it for a few days until the paper retains the tube shape even after it has been unrolled.

Now tape a cardboard tube (the inner from a paper-towel roll will do) to one side of the paper near the central crease.

You must position this so the cardboard tube will be concealed inside the paper when it rolls up by itself.

Fill the cardboard tube with coloured ribbons and you are ready to perform.

Pick the paper tube up from the table and open it out, as shown. Allow it to roll into a tube again, and your audience will believe that you have shown just an ordinary sheet of paper.

Reach into one end of the tube and pull out the ribbons as dramatically as you can.

COIN FOLD

A coin is wrapped in a sheet of paper. A few seconds later the paper is torn up and the coin has vanished.

The secret lies in the way that the paper is folded.

Take a piece of paper about 10 cm (4″) square and place a coin on it slightly below the centre.

Fold the bottom part of the paper up over the coin.

Now fold over the top part of the paper. It is important here not to bring the paper down over the coin but to fold it back, away from you.

Next fold the two sides, also away from you.

It will look as though the coin is well secured inside a small packet. The top edge, however, is open, and it is upon this fact that the trick depends.

Take the paper in one hand, turning it over as you do so.

It is now a simple matter to let the coin slip from the folded packet into your hand.

Tear up the paper, keeping the coin concealed in your hand – and you have achieved yet another miracle!

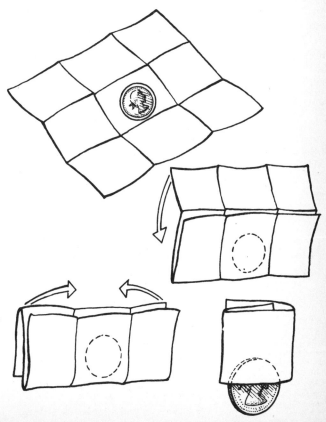

I'VE GOT YOUR NUMBER

Write on a sheet of paper, 'You will end up with the number 1089'. Do not let anyone see what you have written, but fold the paper in half and put it down in full view.

Now ask someone to call out any three-digit number in which all the digits are different. He might, for example, call 147.

There is no need for you to know what the number is provided you can trust the spectator to carry out your instructions and to do some simple arithmetic.

You ask him now to write down the number in reverse. In the example given he would write 741.

You next ask him to subtract the smaller number from the larger. In this example, the answer would be 594.

He must now reverse these figures, and add the two together. Thus, 594 reversed is 495, and 495 plus 594 is 1089.

Ask someone to open the piece of paper, which has been in full view throughout, and read out what is written upon it. Your prediction proves to be correct!

How did you do it? The answer is that it works itself, for the number you predict is always 1089.

Here is another example, to prove the point:

Any three-figure number is chosen, so long as none of the digits is duplicated:

	682
Reverse:	286
Subtract smaller from larger:	396
Reverse:	693
Add together:	1089

THE VANISHING DRINK TRICK

You show a glass tumbler into which you pour some milk. You then announce that you are going to make the tumbler travel across to a box on a nearby table.

The tumbler is covered with a scarf as you ask, 'Would you like it to travel visibly or invisibly?' If the answer is 'Visibly', you take the glass (still under the scarf) across the room and put it in the box.

Should the answer be 'Invisibly', you say, 'If you had replied "Visibly", I would just have taken the glass and placed it in the box, like this.' And you place the glass in the box.

So, no matter which answer you get, you carry out the same actions.

Then you remove the scarf-covered glass from the box as you say, 'I am going to make it travel invisibly.'

You move away from the box. Then, to everyone's surprise, you shake the scarf and show it on both sides. The glass has vanished!

You now cross to the box and remove the glass of milk which has travelled there by magic!

In addition to the glass, milk, scarf and box you will need an extra – identical – scarf and some advance preparation.

From a sheet of cardboard, cut a disc exactly the same size as the mouth of the glass tumbler.

Sew this disc to the centre of the scarf. Place the second scarf on top so the disc is sandwiched between them. Sew the four edges of the scarf together. You can show this on both sides and it looks like an ordinary scarf.

Now to the performance:

Pour some milk into the glass and place the scarf over the top. It must be positioned so that the cardboard disc comes over the mouth of the glass.

Lift the glass, through the scarf, as shown in the illustration. Carry the whole lot over to the box as you ask whether the travelling is to be done visibly or invisibly. Whichever the answer, you place the lot in the box.

You now appear to take the glass out again. But this time, you hold only the hidden disc, and the glass is left in the box.

All you now have to do is throw the scarf into the air and catch it by a corner as it descends. Grasp the opposite corner and show the scarf on both sides.

Now go back to the box and lift out the glass. Take a drink from the glass and take a bow to tumultuous applause.

WHAT'S IN A NAME?

Ask a spectator to shuffle a pack of cards. Then ask him to count off a small number of any cards. This small packet is put aside for the moment.

The spectator next counts off the same number of cards into a second pile. He looks at and remembers the card at the bottom of this second pile, and replaces the pile on top of the pack.

You now take the pack and ask for the spectator's name. 'This is what I want you to do', you say, 'I want you to spell out your name, taking one card off the top of the pack for each letter.' You demonstrate this by spelling out his name, putting one card down for each letter.

When you have finished, you pick up the pile of cards you have just formed and replace them on top of the pack.

Hand the pack to the spectator, but before he starts to spell his name ask him to pick up the pile of cards put aside at the start and place them on top of the pack.

He now spells out his name, one card for each letter.

Ask him the name of the card he memorized. With a dramatic flourish you turn over the top card of the pack – it is his card!

If you follow the above description with a pack of cards in your hands, you will discover that the trick works automatically.

The only thing you have to remember is that the number of letters in the person's name must be greater than the number of cards in the pile put aside at the beginning of the trick.

If the spectator has a short name, you can ask if he has a second Christian name, and add that to the spelling to make certain that you have enough letters to make the trick work.

RED, WHITE AND BLUE

The main items needed for this trick are nine sheets of tissue paper about 15 cm (6″) square; three red, three white and three blue.

You will also need three containers – tins, boxes, or even paper bags will do.

At first reading, this trick may seem rather involved. It is, in fact, very simple. Try it out with the actual props, and, with practice, you'll soon get the hang of it.

Roll each tissue into a ball. Place the three red balls in front (i.e. the side nearest the audience) of the first container; the three white in front of the second container and the three blue in front of the third.

Stand to the right of the table and pick up one of the red balls with your right hand. Place the ball inside the first container. When your hand is completely out of sight, inside the container, simply move the ball so that it rests on the ends of your second and third fingers. Curl these fingers into the palm a little and they will grip the ball (magicians call this a 'finger palm').

Take your hand out of the container with the back of the hand facing the audience. The ball is concealed in this hand, but the audience should believe that you have dropped it inside the container.

Without any hesitation, pick up a white ball and place it in the second container. That, at least, is what you appear to do. What you actually do – once your hand is hidden inside the second container – is to drop the red ball and transfer the white ball to the finger palm position formerly occupied by the red ball.

Remove your hand (with the white ball hidden in the finger palm) and immediately pick up a blue ball. Pretend to place the blue ball in the third container but really repeat the last movement – drop the white ball into the container and finger-palm the blue one.

At this point, your audience should believe you have put a red ball in the first container; a white ball in the second, and a blue ball in the third. What they do not know is that the first container is now empty and you have the blue ball concealed in your right hand, in the finger palm position.

You now change the sequence of actions slightly, but you remain one step ahead of the audience. Pick up the second red ball and appear to drop it into the first container. In reality, you drop the finger-palmed blue ball, and transfer the red ball to the finger palm position.

Next pick up a blue ball; place your hand in the third container; drop the finger-palmed red ball, and then finger-palm the blue ball.

Now pick up a white ball and apparently drop this into the second container, but really leaving the blue ball there.

At the end of this second sequence, you still have a white ball finger-palmed.

Pick up the last red ball, and drop it, together with the palmed white ball, into the first container.

Your hand is empty as you pick up the last white ball and put it into the second container. In the same way, you drop the final blue ball into the third container.

The audience believe that the first container holds three red balls; the second three white balls, and the third three blue balls.

Tip out the contents of each container in turn and each one contains one red, one white and one blue ball.

The actual moves are not difficult, but you must practise them until you can go through the entire sequence without hesitation.

NUMBERED THOUGHTS

A spectator is asked to do some calculations, but the magician works out the answer before the spectator even writes down the various figures.

Hand a pencil and paper to someone in the audience and say that you are going to ask him to do some simple arithmetic. Invite the people on either side of him to check his figures as he goes along.

First the audience is asked to choose any two-figure number. (It could be longer but a small number keeps the arithmetic reasonably simple.)

The spectator writes this down. He is then asked to write date of birth beneath it.

Someone else is asked to call out any famous event and the year that it happened. The year is written down.

Next the spectator is asked to write the age he will be on the last day of the current year.

Finally, he is asked to calculate the number of years since the event chosen, and to write that down.

He must then add up all the figures. When he has finished he announces his answer – only to discover that you wrote down the very same number some time before.

The secret of this trick is simple but also subtly concealed.

As soon as the you hear the two-digit number chosen by the audience at the start you know what the final answer is going to be, and you can write it down before the spectator puts any more figures on his paper.

All you have to do is carry in your head twice the number of the year in which you are performing. In 1990, for example, this number will be 3980 (2 × 1990).

When the two-digit number is called, you add this

to the number you already have in mind. Thus, if the number was 47 the final answer (in 1990) will be 4025 (3980 + 45).

Let us work through an example of a complete performance using this number. We will also assume that the spectator was born in 1972, and that the chosen event is the Coronation of Queen Elizabeth II (1953).

This is what the spectator writes:

45	(number chosen by audience)
1972	(year of spectator's birth)
1953	(year of Coronation)
18	(spectator's age on last day of the year)
37	(years since Coronation)

4025 TOTAL

This total tallies with yours!

If you look at the figures closely, you will realize that the total of the spectator's year of birth and his age will always add up to 1990 (or whatever year the performance takes place). Similarly, the date of the event and the number of years since it occurred will also add up to the same figure. The only number you cannot possibly know in advance is the one selected by the audience; as soon as you know that, you know what the answer will be!

RISING PENCIL

Many a magician has made his or her reputation with this trick. As with most magic, the means of achieving it are quite simple, but to an audience it appears to be really magical.

You will need a length of dark thread. You will have to experiment to get the correct length, but you should find that 60 centimetres (about two feet) is about right. Attach one end of the thread to one of your coat buttons. To the free end of the thread stick a small blob of plasticine. Put the plasticined end in a convenient pocket.

When you are ready to perform you will need to borrow a long pencil and an empty bottle. You can, of course, do the trick with your own pencil and bottle, but magic is usually much more convincing if you borrow ordinary objects from your spectators.

Have the pencil examined and then handed back to you.

Now ask for the bottle to be examined.

While everyone's attention is on the bottle, put your hand in your pocket; take out the plasticined end of the thread, and press the plasticine against the unsharpened end of the pencil.

Take back the bottle and drop the pencil into it – plasticine end first.

The illustration shows the position at this stage of the trick.

Hold the bottle in one hand and make mystic passes over it with your free hand. As you do this, move the bottle forward slightly. The thread will tauten and the pencil will rise up out of the bottle.

Bring the bottle towards you again, and the pencil will fall back into the bottle.

After doing this a few times, take the pencil out of the bottle and secretly pull off the plasticine before you drop the pencil on to the table. You can, if you wish, hand both pencil and bottle out to the audience for examination once again. But you will find that there is no need to invite them as several people will want to take a look without any prompting from you.

RING OF CONFIDENCE
This trick uses exactly the same thread set-up as for 'Rising Pencil', described on page 75.

You borrow a pencil and attach the plasticine to it as before. You can do this while asking someone to lend you a finger ring.

Hold the pencil by the pointed end and drop the ring over the other end. The illustration shows the position of everything at this stage.

If you now move your hand forward, the thread will tauten and the ring will to rise up the pencil.

Hand the pencil and ring back to their respective owners – and you have accomplished yet another miracle.

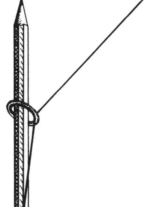

USING YOUR GREY MATTER

You state that you and your assistant have developed an amazing ability that you would like to demonstrate.

While your assistant is out of the room, you ask someone in the audience to choose any object in the room.

Your assistant returns and, without saying a word, you point to several objects.

Even though you do not speak, nor do you even look at your assistant, he reacts as soon as you point to the chosen object.

By the time you have repeated this a couple of times, everyone will believe that you can indeed read each other's minds.

The trick is accomplished by means of a simple code.

First, both you and your assistant must remember the single word 'GREY'.

This word is used to indicate the order of three colours as follows:

```
G  R  e  Y
r  e     e
e  d     l
e        l
n        o
         w
```

On the first demonstration, you point to a green object immediately before the chosen object. Your assistant knows at once that the next is the item chosen.

If you want to repeat the trick, point to a red object before the chosen one, and do it the third time using yellow.

If you want to continue this demonstration of uncanny mind control, you simply repeat the sequence of green, red and yellow.

IT MUST BE MIND-READING

Occasionally, when doing the last trick, you will come across someone who says: 'Can I point to the objects?'

If you agree, the code from 'Using Your Grey Matter' becomes impossible, so it is wise for you and your assistant to know this version. The effect is exactly the same, but anyone can point to the objects in any order. Your assistant can still identify the selected items, without you saying a word.

The secret code in this case is any simple but unobtrusive natural movement that you have agree in advance.

It could be something as simple as putting your hand in a pocket.

The spectator points to various objects. As soon as you put your hand in your pocket, your assistant knows that the spectator is pointing to the chosen object.

If you want to perform this trick several times in succession, you can easily devise a sequence of different signals.

It is important that each signal is natural and not obvious to anyone watching you closely. It is also important that your assistant must not appear to be looking at you all the time.

TABLE LIFTING

You place your hand on a small table. Much to everyone's surprise, the table adheres to your hand and is lifted from the floor.

This trick is often used by people who claim to have supernatural powers; but you can duplicate the effect with a little cunning.

You need a light table (obviously choosing one which is not very valuable). In the centre of the table-top, hammer a nail. Hammer it so that its head projects only slightly.

You will also need to wear a prepared finger ring. On the underside (palm side) of the ring you have cut a semicircular notch.

Bring your hand over the table top and secretly engage the nail head in the notch of the ring as you do so.

When you lift your hand, the table will rise with it, and you will be able to move it around in a most mysterious manner.

LUCKY THIRTEEN

The best way to learn this trick is to follow the instructions with a pack of cards in your hands.

First remove the Jokers and then shuffle the pack.

Turn over the top card. Using the pips on that card as your starting point, place cards on it face up until you reach thirteen. Thus, if the first card was a Seven, you would place six other cards on top of it counting, 'Eight, nine, ten, eleven, twelve, thirteen.'

Turn over the next card to start another pile in the same way. Let us assume this next card is a Ten. You then place cards face up on it counting 'Eleven, twelve, thirteen.'

Continue making piles of cards until you have gone right through the pack. An Ace counts as one; Jack as eleven; Queen as twelve, and King as thirteen. Thus, if a King is the first card of a pile, there is no need to put any more cards on top; instead, you turn over the next card to start another pile.

It is possible that you may not be able to get rid of the entire pack in this manner. If not, just keep the odd cards in your hand for the moment.

Now turn all the piles face down, and ask someone to pick two piles. Turn the top card of each chosen pile face up.

Next ask for a third pile to be chosen, but do not turn over the top card just yet.

Gather together all the cards except those in the three selected piles and add them to any odd cards you may have had left over.

In your head, add together the pips on the two cards that have been turned over. Let us assume these are a Five and an Eight – so your total will be thirteen. Add ten to this, making twenty-three.

Now count the cards you hold in your hands. From the number you hold subtract the figure that you are thinking of (23 in the example above). Your answer will be the number of pips on the face down card on top of the third selected pile.

Point out that no one could possibly know the value of this card. Call out the answer you have arrived at, and have someone turn the card over. You are absolutely correct!

The trick is based on a mathematical principle, and therefore works automatically. It is wise, however, to try it out a few times in advance to make sure that you understand the complete procedure.

PURE MIND-READING

All you need is a pack of cards, a handkerchief and a little advance thinking. This consists of remembering the top three cards of the pack.

Spread the cards out face up, to show that they are all different.

Close up the cards and cover them with the handkerchief. As soon as the pack is hidden from view, turn it upside down beneath the handkerchief.

Ask someone to step forward and lift off part of the pack, holding this cut-off portion through the material.

Bring the bottom part of the pack from under the handkerchief, but turn it over before bringing it back into view.

The spectators will think that this is the bottom half of the pack. But it is not – it is the original top half.

Have three spectators each take one card from the top and look at them.

Since these are the three cards you memorized earlier it is an easy matter to pretend to read the minds of the spectators, and reveal the names of the cards.

TWO HEADS ARE BETTER THAN ONE

In this trick, a coin is shown to have a head on both sides.

But the coin is quite ordinary, and the effect is accomplished by some crafty sleight of hand.

Follow these directions and the illustrations with a coin in your hand.

Place the coin on the palm of your right hand, with the head side showing (a).

Move your right hand sharply to the right so that the coin slides off and drops on to your left hand (b) (c).

As the coin falls, turn your right hand over (d).

The coin falls down on to your left hand, and your right hand slaps down on top of it (e).

Lift your right hand to show that the coin has a head on the other side.

You must practise these movements until you can do them quickly and smoothly. It should look as though you simply turned your hand over to show both sides of the coin. However, the coin does not turn over at all.

Practise doing this trick with both hands. You can then pass the coin back to the right hand – and there will still be a head showing. To the people watching, it appears that the coin really does have two heads!

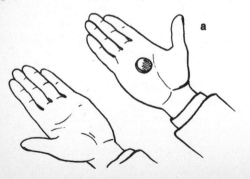

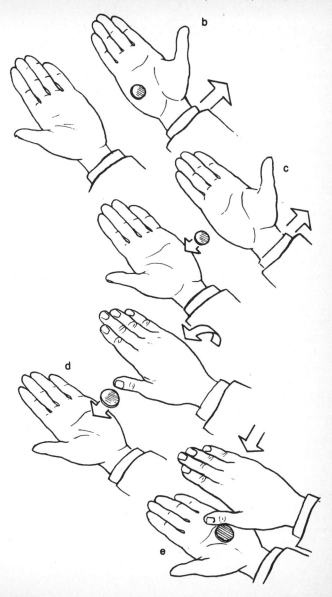

SPELL IT OUT

Prior to your performance of this trick, you must arrange a pack of cards in the following order. The suits do not matter:

9, J, 5, A, K, K, 7, 2, 6, Q, 10, A, 3, 3, 8, K, 8, 7, 4, 2, A, A, 7, 5, 9, 2, J, 6, Q, 6, 10, 3, 3, 7, 4, 2, 8, J, 4, 8, J, 4, Q, K, 9, 5, 10, Q, 10, 9, 6, 5.

If the pack is face down, a Nine will be on the top and a Five at the bottom.

Put the pack in its case, and you are ready to show an amazing feat.

In your performance, you remove the pack from its case, and then take the top card and place it on the bottom, as you say 'A'.

The next card is placed on the bottom as you say 'C'.

Place the next card on the bottom, as you say 'E'.

You have thus spelled out the word ACE, transferring one card to the bottom of the pack for each letter. Turn over the top card of the pack – it is an Ace!

Discard the Ace and then spell 'Two' in the same way, transferring one card from top to bottom for each letter. The next card will be a Two!

You continue in this way all through the pack, spelling out cards in the correct sequence.

THE EGG-LAYING HANDKERCHIEF

This remarkable handkerchief will enable you to produce eggs from nowhere.

To prepare it, you will need a handkerchief, some thread and an egg. It is best to use a blown egg or a china egg (available from pet shops, joke shops or magic shops).

The egg is attached to the centre of one side of the

Secrets of the Professionals · 85

handkerchief with the thread, as shown in the first illustration (a).

You will also need a box or some other receptacle.

At the start, the handkerchief is flat on the table with the egg hanging down behind (b).

Pick up the handkerchief by the two front corners (marked A and B in the illustrations).

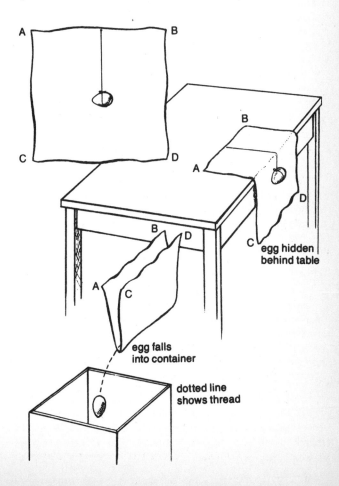

Carry it towards the receptacle, and fold it in half as shown. Turn the handkerchief on one side and allow the egg to roll from it, into the receptacle (c).

Let go of corners C and D and, holding corners A and B, lift the handkerchief away from the receptacle. The egg comes away as well, hidden behind the handkerchief.

By repeating the above movements as many times as you wish, you can produce eggs *ad infinitum*.

When you (and your audience) have had enough, tip up the receptacle. It is completely empty!

EXTRA-SENSORY CARDCEPTION

A pack of cards is shuffled a few times and handed to the magician. The magician holds the pack behind his back for a second or two, before bringing it forward again.

He holds the cards in front of him in such a way that the audience can see the bottom card but the magician cannot.

Then he takes the pack behind his back, removes the card just named, and tosses it face up on to the table.

He brings the pack to the front once more and again names the new bottom card which he cannot possibly see. Repeating the previous actions, he then tosses this card face up on to the table.

This is continued through most of the pack, the magician showing, naming and then throwing out each bottom card in turn.

This trick can be performed with any pack of cards, which can be well shuffled by any spectator. As you – the magician – take back the pack, you manage to take a quick glimpse of the bottom card. You must do this without anyone noticing.

Take the cards behind your back and secretly cut some off, reverse them, and place them back on the pack. The pack now has half (or fewer) of the cards facing one way, and the rest facing the other.

Bring the pack forward and hold it up in front of you. The original bottom card (the one you glimpsed) is facing the audience. You name it.

As you do so, note the card facing you.

Take the pack behind your back; remove the card you have just named, bring it forward and throw it on to the table. Now reverse the pack in your hand so that the card you have just remembered will be facing the audience when you bring the pack forward again.

Call out this card and remember the card facing you.

Again hold the pack behind your back, and carry out the same procedure as before.

If, at the beginning, you had divided the pack exactly in half you could go through the entire pack naming cards in this way.

It is, however, better to reverse only about a quarter of the pack and to name cards only until the back of one faces you, at which point you stop. You thus create the impression that you could go through all the cards if you so wished. This also means that, at the end of the trick, you can bring the rest of the pack forward and, since all the cards are facing the same way, there is no clue as to how you accomplished this fantastic feat of mental perception.

IT'S WRITTEN IN THE ASHES

A card is chosen by a spectator and its identity is written on a piece of paper. The paper is burned and the ashes rubbed across the performer's bare arm. As if by magic, the name of the chosen card appears on the performer's arm!

There are two secrets to this trick. The first is that the card is not freely chosen (although this appears to be the case), and the second is that the performer's arm has been specially treated before the performance.

Let us deal with the performer's arm first. All you have to do is take a pointed piece of soap and write on your arm 6D (to indicate the Six of Diamonds), or whichever card you decide to use.

To get a spectator to choose the card you want him to, while apparently giving him a free choice is what magicians call 'forcing'. There are lots of ways of forcing a card, but for this trick we will use one of the simplest.

Take a pack of cards and place the Six of Diamonds (or whichever card you decide to use) ninth from the top.

During your performance, ask for someone to call out any number between ten and twenty. Let us assume that he calls out sixteen. Count off sixteen cards from the top of the pack.

Point out that the number is composed of two digits, a one and a six. One plus six equals seven, so, from the pile of cards you have just dealt, you count off seven cards. The next card is placed to one side as 'the card freely chosen'.

Believe it or not, but that card will be the card you placed at the ninth position from the top. (This method works for any number between ten and twenty).

Ask someone to write the name of the selected card on a piece of paper. The paper is then burned and the ashes rubbed over your arm, where you soaped it earlier. Some of the ashes will stick to the soap, and thus the identity of the chosen card is revealed!

DISAPPEARING COIN

A coin is placed in a handkerchief. When the handkerchief is shaken out, the coin has vanished.

To do this trick you will need, in addition to a coin and a handkerchief, a small elastic band.

Before showing the trick, secretly slip the elastic band over the thumb and first two fingers of your left hand.

Pick up the handkerchief and drape it directly over the fingers holding the elastic band.

Take the coin and push it into the handkerchief, making sure that it goes into the fingers holding the elastic band beneath the handkerchief.

Allow the elastic band to slip off your fingers. You can now throw the handkerchief up in the air and it will seem that the coin has vanished. It is actually concealed within the folds of the handkerchief, held in place by the elastic band. Provided that you handle the handkerchief normally no one will realize this.

RICE SUSPENSION

This trick comes from India and it takes a certain knack which can only be obtained by trial and error.

You need a light bowl, enough rice to fill the bowl, and a broad-bladed knife.

It is important that the neck of the bowl is considerably narrower than the bowl itself.

Fill the bowl to the brim with rice. Tap the sides to settle the rice, and then add more rice to fill it right to the top.

Plunge the blade of the knife into the centre of the rice. Now stab the knife up and down a few times. As you do this, you will find that it gets harder and harder to do. Eventually the rice will grip the knife so firmly that you will not be able to pull it out. When you lift the knife the bowl will rise with it!

Place the bowl back on the table. Twist the knife slightly and you will be able to remove it from the rice quite easily.

TURNOVER TRICKERY

A selected card reverses itself in the pack in this trick.

Before you perform, secretly turn over the bottom card of the pack so that it is face up.

Begin by spreading out the cards face down, and ask a spectator to take any card. Be careful not to show the reversed card.

Ask the spectator to show his card to the rest of the audience. While he is doing this, close the pack and then secretly turn it over in your hands.

Have the card pushed, face down, into the pack. Because of the reversed card on top everyone will think that the rest of the pack is also face down.

Now announce that you are going to try to find the chosen card in an unusual way.

Hold the pack behind your back; turn the reversed card over and replace it. Then turn the whole pack over so that all the cards, with the exception of the chosen card somewhere in the centre, are face down.

Tell your audience you have found the chosen card, taken it out of the pack and put it back face up.

Place the cards on the table and ask for the name of the chosen card. Spread the cards out. In the middle, there is one card face up – it is the chosen card.

THROUGH THE LEGS

This trick uses exactly the same movements as Vanishing Coin (p. 60) but the coin doesn't vanish. Instead it passes through your legs!

Follow the procedure of the previous trick up to the point where you close your right hand and the coin stays secretly concealed in your left. This time, however, you do not drop the coin into your pocket but keep it hidden in your hand.

Bring your right hand down to touch the outside of your right knee and your left hand down to touch the outside of your left knee.

Tap your right hand against the right knee and then open your hand. The coin has vanished.

Tap the left hand against the left knee and open that hand. The coin is now seen in your left hand. It appears to have passed through your legs by magic.

LIVING AND DEAD

Five blank pieces of card and five pencils are handed out to members of your audience.

Four people are each asked to write the name of any living person on their card. The fifth person is asked to write the name of any famous person who is dead.

The cards are then sealed in envelopes and the envelopes mixed up.

You take the envelopes one by one and concentrate hard. Eventually you hold up one envelope and announce that it is the one which holds the name of the dead person.

The envelope is opened – and you are shown to be correct.

The secret of this reputation-making effect is quite simple:

After the names are written and the cards collected, it is their positioning in the envelopes that is important.

You must place the cards bearing the names of living people into their envelopes horizontally. The dead person card is placed in a vertical position inside its envelope.

The envelopes can now be mixed up. All you have to do is to feel them in turn. It is quite easy to pick out the one containing the vertical card.

IT'S WRITTEN IN THE CARDS

A pack of cards is well shuffled and then spread out face down on a table. The magician takes one card at random, writes something on it and drops it into a box.

A spectator picks any one of the face down cards and drops it into the box also.

The two cards are removed from the box. Across the magician's card is written 'Three of Diamonds'. The spectator's card is shown. It is the Three of Diamonds!

You will have to use a whole pack of cards to do this trick – and you will need a new pack each time you show it – but the effect is so fantastic that the expense is well worth it.

Remove from the pack the Three of Diamonds (or whatever card you decide to use). Put a small pencil mark on the back of it so you can identify it later.

On the face of every other card in the pack write 'Three of Diamonds'. Write near the bottom edge of each card so you can fan out the cards but keep the writing hidden. The pack thus appears quite ordinary.

Reassemble the pack, find a suitable box, and you are ready to perform.

Shuffle the cards (if you are really brave you can get one of the audience to shuffle the cards), and then spread them out, face down, on the table.

While you are spreading them, you are searching for the marked Three of Diamonds.

Casually remove it and pretend to write on it (in actual fact you write nothing on the card). Place this card, without showing its face, into the box.

Now ask for any one of the other cards to be selected. Since they all have 'Three of Diamonds' written on the face, it doesn't matter which card is chosen. Drop this card, face unseen, into the box. Gather up the rest of the cards, making certain that no one sees that they have something written on them.

Take the two cards from the box, and hold up the one on which is written 'Three of Diamonds'. Show it as if it were the card on which you made your prediction.

Emphasize the fact that the spectator had an absolutely free choice. Now turn over the other card (which everyone will think was the the one that the spectator chose) and reveal that it is the card you predicted – the Three of Diamonds!

FLY THE FLAG

Three handkerchiefs of different colours are wrapped in a sheet of newspaper. After the magic words have been spoken the paper is torn open and – hey, presto! – the handkerchiefs have changed into a flag.

You prepare for this trick as follows:

Fold the flag and place it on the centre of a sheet of newspaper. Take a second sheet of newspaper and place it on top of the first, and over the flag. Glue the two sheets of paper so that the flag is well hidden in the envelope thus formed.

When perfoming, you show the three handkerchiefs and wrap them up in your prepared sheet.

All you now have to do is tear into the bundle you hold – and pull out the flag. It is as simple as that!

Naturally, the colours of the handkerchiefs you use should match those of the flag.

INDEX

THE FAMILY MATTERS SERIES